Hiking and Backpacking
with Dogs

Linda B. Mullally

FALCONGUIDES

GUILFORD, CONNECTICUT
HELENA, MONTANA

AN IMPRINT OF ROWMAN & LITTLEFIELD

Dedicated to our canine friends Lobo, Shiloh, Moses, Sky, Schnapps, and Coffee, who are bounding on the trails across Rainbow Bridge

FALCONGUIDES®

Copyright © 2014 by Morris Book Publishing, LLC

Backpacker is a registered trademark of Cruz Bay Publishing, Inc.
FalconGuides is an imprint of Rowman & Littlefield.
Falcon, FalconGuides, and Outfit Your Mind are registered trademarks of Rowman & Littlefield.

All photos by David Mullally unless noted otherwise.

Distributed by NATIONAL BOOK NETWORK

Library of Congress Cataloging-in-Publication data is available on file.

ISBN 978-0-7627-8265-9

Printed in the United States of America

Contents

Acknowledgments

I trace my love of the outdoors to growing up in Trois-Rivières, Québec, where my backyard was the shores of the Saint Maurice and Saint Lawrence Rivers. My earliest memories of hiking and snowshoeing are of following my grandmother on forested trails behind the modest cabin my grandparents called home on the edge of French Canada wilderness.

I was six years old when I discovered the unparalleled joy of loving and being loved by a dog, when a miniature silver French Poodle I named Sophie came into my life. She was my first companion in outdoor adventuring. From that moment, partly through fate and my maternal grandmother's First Nation (Native American) genetic legacy, there never has been another place on the planet that has made my heart and soul feel more at home than on a mountain trail with a pack on my back and a dog at my side.

From poodles and doodles to huskies and hybrids, four-legged companions have enhanced every nature walk and backpacking trip while deepening my connection with the natural world.

I want to express my gratitude to several people, agencies, and businesses for their contributions to this book.

My husband and talented photographer, David, has shared my boundless enthusiasm for adventure and enhanced all my articles and books with his vivid photography.

Friends (old and new) trusted me with their cherished photogenic four-legged family members as their "doggie nanny" at home as well as their dogs' caretaker and trainer on the road and on the trail.

George Bishop, DVM, executive committee member of the American Veterinary Medical Association (AVMA), has provided thirty years of sound professional advice, while Suzi Blufford, a dog trainer for over forty years with seven breed championships and an AKC judge, has helped shepherd me and countless other initially clueless dog owners through our dogs' chaotic but formative puppy phase. And Pluis Davern, a guru of dog obedience, taught me that training your dog also means respecting your dog.

REI, Pet Food Express, Wolf Packs, and Ruffwear were gracious enough to let my trail companions test-hike gear and accessories.

Introduction

The moment of truth came when a friend told me she had never seen a dog spring on all fours from the floor onto the coffee table like our two pups did. I had to admit that Lobo and Shiloh exhibited a lot of behaviors I had never observed in any of the other dogs I had owned or known.

Thus began an intense investigation of our two dogs' background beyond the breeder's romantic tales of authentic "Native" dog rescue and breed preservation and denials of any recent wolf or coyote breeding.

Weeks of phone calls, letters, and networking with other "Native" dog owners helped my husband, David, and me connect the dots and follow the trail to a breeder in South Dakota.

The breeder confirmed what had become increasingly clear over the last few months and identified our dogs as offspring of her Husky/coyote breeding stock. They shared some of the characteristics and certainly the appearance of the original "Plains Indian dog" but were in no way "authentic" or "descendants" of these legendary travois-pulling dogs associated with Native American nomadic life.

I had ignored all my instincts' red flags and naively swallowed a story that changed my husband's and my life for sixteen years. By the time the lights went on, we were committed to two of these unusual canines and had contributed to perpetuating a pyramid-style dog scheme. Now we had to figure out how to reshape our lives to meet the needs of these two adorable and intriguing four-legged hellions.

We embarked on a sixteen-year adventure with Lobo and Shiloh. We redesigned our home and our lives for mutual adaptation and cohabitation. When even a fenced yard was too close to our neighbors' chickens for comfort and our dogs' singing sounded more like "screaming" to another neighbor, we moved to ten acres at the edge of the Ventana Wilderness. We ran or hiked everyone's edge off at dawn every morning. We traded state and national parks that prohibit dogs for dog-friendly regional open space, national forests, BLM land, and Canadian parks.

It was the best of times hiking and backpacking in the backcountry, seeing and appreciating the natural world through our dogs' hyper-alert senses, and the worst of times in tight civilized corners where their strong prey instinct endangered tiny, fluffy things at the end of leashes.

Not knowing any coyote hybrid wranglers who would house-sit, we took few trips without the dogs. On the few occasions when we traveled guiltily *sans chiens,* we boarded them reluctantly in our veterinarian's care.

I would never repeat the experience, nor do I regret it. If life with Lobo and Shiloh was an intensely challenging

The author with Lobo and Shiloh on an Eastern Sierra adventure

and sometimes frustrating exploit, life was also richer because of sharing a unique bond with two free spirits who took us on a personal journey with nature in California and across the USA and Canada. They inspired me to share the rewards of hiking and backpacking with a dog in three books and the joy of traveling with a four-legged companion in *Dog Fancy*'s first travel column.

Hiking with Lobo and Shiloh has made me a better dog owner and a more responsible and aware steward of the land no matter where I happen to be wandering on the planet.

Since their passing over Rainbow Bridge, David and I have continued to introduce friends' dogs to the joy of the trail and most recently Gypsy, the little ten-year-old Australian Cattle Dog / Chihuahua we inherited in the summer of 2012. In 2013, with Gypsy's and David's approval, I will begin my quest for the Husky pup I hope will complement our pack by the summer of 2014.

ABOUT THIS BOOK

Whether you step off a paved path for a mile or retreat for several overnights, there's nothing like filling your lungs with fresh air, reveling in scenic open spaces, and delighting in your dog's exuberance in the natural world.

The author with Gypsy on his first backcountry hike

Some of your best memories will be backpacking with your dog.

This book was inspired by my lifelong love affair with dogs and hiking. It is a pleasure and a privilege to share my experience and others' expert knowledge to offer tips on choosing and training a dog to maximize the joys and benefits of safe hiking and backpacking with your dog. Newcomers to outdoor recreating with a dog will appreciate my step-by-step approach to the trail with a suggested training schedule, checklists, and helpful resources.

If you are an outdoor enthusiast with miles already under your boots and paws, the book will complement and reinforce some of what you may already know while giving you some fresh insights on how to enhance your relationship and partnership with your best friend and trail companion.

Chapter One

10 Good Reasons to Hike and Backpack with Your Dog

1. Hiking/backpacking is a healthy, noncompetitive, and inexpensive form of outdoor recreation. It is the perfect escape from urban stress and the daily grind while providing an opportunity for you and pooch to reset your metabolisms to "fit."

2. As a dog owner you have the privilege of having a live-in natural hiking companion who will enhance the experience in a unique way.

3. Your dog's innate curiosity will make you notice and appreciate more of the natural world around you.

4. Your dog's alertness and intuition can give you an added sense of security.

5. Hiking and backpacking provides time for quality bonding between you and your dog, free of daily distractions and demands.

6. Hiking is a natural and enjoyable way for people and dogs to stay fit. The running up a dirt trail, leaping over streams, and climbing on boulders that keep a dog's spirit soaring and her body agile, trim, and toned can also work for you.

7. Hiking and the training regimen involved to keep your dog in good form can be excellent prevention for several physical and behavioral disorders and in some cases may help reduce the symptoms of other ailments. As in humans, obesity can trigger more serious health problems such as heart attack, high blood pressure, diabetes, or even arthritis.

8. Hiking can also benefit your dog mentally. The natural smells, sights, and sounds off the beaten track are invigorating and rejuvenating for both of you.

9. Hiking can help dogs reduce destructive behavior or depression associated with boredom.

10. Regular exercise in the great outdoors can help mellow out high-strung dogs and dogs prone to overt dominance and aggression.

Fit or Fat?

To determine how fit your dog is, use this simple rule: You should be able to feel your dog's ribs when you run your hands along her sides (feel them, not see them). Stress on a dog's joints from carrying extra weight can also exacerbate preexisting conditions such as hip dysplasia. The exercise from hiking can help keep your dog trim and strengthen muscles that support the hips.

Chapter Two

Different Dogs for Different Hikes

The domestic dog has been traced back to the wolf, which roamed throughout North America, Europe, Asia, and India over twelve thousand years ago. Dog's ancestral instinct to hunt and bond with his pack has been the key to centuries of successful selective breeding for performing specialized functions. There are over four hundred dog breeds recognized around the world, varying in size, appearance, and abilities. From the largest (Irish Wolfhound) to the smallest (Chihuahua), all retain a strong to slight instinctive link to their wild roots.

At one end of the spectrum, natural dog breeds (dogs with primitive stock) demonstrate more of their wild ancestors' characteristics and instincts. Typically, these medium-size, prick-eared, pointed-muzzled dogs have balanced proportions for speed on the hunt. Alert, aloof, agile, and energetic with a striking intelligent gaze, these dogs are seductive.

This breed type has potentially excellent qualities as an exciting hiking companion, but it is a poor choice for the first-time dog owner. Their strong independent but sensitive temperaments require training "finesse" that balances firmness with patience and intense bonding while reinforcing impulse control without breaking their free spirit. They require "purpose" through daily exercise and mental stimulation to keep their energy focused, preventing the restlessness and boredom that is sure to get them into trouble and irritate their owner. Australian Cattle Dogs (aka Queensland Heelers), Basenjis, and Pharaoh Hounds as well as thicker-coated northern breeds like Huskies and Norwegian Elkhounds are examples of more primitive stock.

First-time dog owners should not choose a dog with too much primitive blood.

I cannot talk about primitive breeds without mentioning hybrids (wolf, coyote, or dingo mixes). Their exotic wild look makes heads turn and speaks to the free spirit and primal energy in each of us. While some dog breeds are challenging, true hybrids are unfairly caught between two worlds and unfit for either.

Hybrids are often misunderstood and unmanageable. Unless they find a home with someone willing to devote his or her life to meeting the animal's psychological and physical activity needs, they are doomed to a life of abuse under human inaptitude or die from a rancher's bullet.

Some dog owners pride themselves on the ratio of wild blood (wolf or coyote) to domestic (German Shepherd or Malamute) in their dog. Whether these owners know what they are talking about, few people can give a hybrid quality of life while guaranteeing the safety of their dog and their neighbors' livestock and/or pets.

In general, hybrids, controversial domestic breeds, or any individual dog labeled "unpredictable" does not belong on the hiking trail or in social settings where people, pets, or wildlife will be at risk of injury or worse. In the case of dogs prone to aggression, the distinction must be made between dogs born with trigger temperaments and those that develop bad tempers due to a traumatic start in life, lack of exercise, or lack of social stimulation.

This brings us to the debate over nature vs. nurture. If a dog's distressed disposition is determined to be a result of the latter (conditioning vs. a genetic condition), hiking and backpacking can be a great adjunct therapy for modifying and mellowing behavior. Medication can sometimes mitigate hard-wired neurotic behavior, while an exercise and gradual socialization regimen can lead to happiness on the trail for many dogs.

If you are on the threshold of dog ownership, why not focus on the many socially accepted and embraced breeds and mixes, and avoid the controversy and stress of Pit Bulls. The most important characteristic in a dog is "temperament."

At the other end of the canine spectrum are those dogs that breeding has stripped of their original practical functions of herding, hunting, guarding, or retrieving to transform them more into "companion" or "lap" dogs depending on size. Companion breeds like Yorkshire Terriers, Poodles, Chihuahuas, and variations thereof can be surprisingly hardy hikers.

There is a wide range of breeds in the middle, including the hounds, sporting dogs, and working dogs. All have their strengths and weaknesses. But the more "trendy" a breed becomes, the more susceptible it is to suffer from physical and psychological frailties. Less-responsible breeders see popularity as an opportunity to make more cash, and breeding gets amped, pouring more genetically unsound dogs into the gene pool.

Temperament should be at the top of the list when choosing a trail dog.

The popularity of a breed and recognition by kennel clubs for "show" purposes, emphasizing certain arbitrary physical attributes, or "conformation," for the show ring, can also result in a breed being weakened, with increased cases of hip dysplasia, allergies, strange skin conditions, and neurotic behavior. When you hear that mutts are often healthier and smarter than purebreds, it says something about "natural" selection.

Among the new breed flavors that have come under the spotlight in the last decade, the Poodle-infused combos are *so far* proving to be a generally successful experiment, especially in the medium-size format. The "poo" and "doodle" designs usually have shed-free coats and combine the smarts and athleticism of Poodles with the affability of Cocker Spaniels, Labradors, and Golden Retrievers.

TRAITS FOR THOUGHT

» Be aware that thick-coated dogs overheat more easily. The woolly-coated Husky is an example of a beautiful trail-loving companion in cool weather but can be a perpetual grooming nightmare.

» Thick coats on any dog get heavier when wet and can turn a tired dog into a drowning dog.

» Black coated dogs absorb more heat.

» Long coats and curly coats can be Velcro coats for burrs and foxtails (a trail trim is the answer).

» Thin-coated to hairless dogs may need to be protected from sun and cold.

» Short-muzzled dogs, such as Pugs, Boxers, and Bulldogs, cannot cool air efficiently through their short sinus passages, so they tend to overheat during exertion.

» Short legs mean slower and shorter hikes; Corgis and Dachshunds are examples.

» Giant breeds like Bernese Mountain Dogs and St. Bernards mature more slowly physically. Beware of joint problems if tackling stairs and hills too young (before twelve to eighteen months).

Medium-size Poodle mixes like Cockapoos and Labradoodles have good dispositions and stamina.

> » Some breeds are naturally yappy, a character trait in direct opposition to backcountry solitude.

THE COMPATIBILITY QUIZ

When looking to add a dog to your pack (family) with hiking and/or backpacking in mind, it is essential to consider the breed's characteristics, including size, build, stamina, and temperament.

Be realistic about your own personality and life-style "off the trail"—not just your outdoor interests and trail ambitions. The following questions could be the key to a happy, mutually gratifying pairing.

- » Do you have children? Some dogs are more tolerant than others of "family" dynamics.
- » Do you rent or own? If you rent, make sure your landlord allows pets.
- » Is there another dog in the house? Some breeds are more territorial than others.
- » What is the size of your indoor living space? An upstairs studio apartment may work for a Papillion but would be tight with a Rottweiler.
- » Do you have access to a secure ground-floor outdoor space (yard or courtyard)? Tying a dog to a chain is cruel and promotes aggressive behavior.
- » Do you have time to train and care for a dog and meet his daily needs for exercise, mental stimulation, and emotional connection off the trail? For example, Labs are content retrieving sticks and balls on a lawn, but Huskies need large territories to run.
- » Do you have access to a park, open space, or water where your dog can romp or swim to maintain his hiking form and beat the boredom between hikes?
- » Do you have the time or the budget for a dog with high-maintenance grooming requirements as well as the inevitable veterinary care bills?
- » Do you have the patience and schedule flexibility to commit to the needs of a puppy,

or is an already housebroken and trained adult dog more suitable to your lifestyle?

» Do you have allergies? If so, narrow your search to breeds that don't shed.

DO YOUR HOMEWORK

If you have a breed or breed type in mind, talk to people who live with the breed and read about it. Talk to dog trainers and breeders, and speak to your veterinarian about his experience with the breed or breed type as patients. What common conditions are they treated for, if any? Being a spectator at a couple obedience classes will also give you a sense of how different breeds and/or mixes respond to training.

MATCHMAKING

Once you have narrowed down the breed, where do you find that future hiking companion?

Breeders

If you want a purebred, start interviewing breeders. Word of mouth is the best source for a reputable breeder. You also can get the names of breeders from veterinary offices, kennel clubs, and breed rescue clubs. Websites and dog magazines should not be your only sources.

The right breeder will be concerned with a good match between dog and owner rather than a fast buck. He will interview you carefully and forthrightly.

The breeder's contract should include a clause that guarantees the health of the pup and certifications that clear the parents of genetic defects.

An individual who breeds for the love of dogs will encourage contact and progress reports on how your pup is doing and will be available to find the dog a new home if necessary. That breeder will keep puppies with their littermates for at least eight weeks, during which time he provides them with human companionship and regular exposure to household activity. Beware of breeders who seem eager to unload their puppies sooner.

The clean, comfortable whelping box or doggie nursery should be in the breeder's home and reflect that the breeder cares about the animals. Ask to meet the pup's parents, as their appearance and disposition will tell you a lot about the puppies. If the male is not available, ask to talk to his owner and veterinarian.

Never hesitate to ask for references and contact information for other puppy buyers. Find a reputable breeder within a distance you will be willing and comfortable to drive for home visits and to pick up your pup.

Do not buy a dog online to save money, and do not let a breeder talk you into putting your pup on an airplane. Transporting a pet by air should only be done if absolutely necessary and on nonstop direct flights.

Breed Rescue Clubs

Many breed clubs have a rescue network for their own breed. The network is a support system for dog owners who are no longer able to keep the dog. This is a good source for someone who wants to bypass the trials and tribulations of puppy chewing and housebreaking by adopting a more mature dog that has a known history and extensive training.

Animal Shelters

Visit your community animal shelter. Many wonderful purebreds and an even greater number of mixed breeds that deserve a good home are abandoned, lost, or given up to shelters daily. Some mixed breeds benefit from natural selection and display the best traits of their breed potpourri.

Be aware that some shelter dogs have had a traumatic start in life and require extra devotion and loving patience on their way to becoming great companions. If you find a dog that tugs at your heartstrings, get as much information as you can about the dog's breed or mix, background, and the reason the dog was given up for adoption. Talk to the shelter caretakers about their observations. Take the dog outside, away from the chaos and stress of the shelter environment, to interact with him and evaluate his disposition and your chemistry with him.

Pet Stores

Support your local pet store by shopping for products and supplies, not live animals. Some pet stores are a pipeline for backyard breeders and puppy mills. Reputable breeders do not supply pet stores with puppies.

Advertisements

Newspapers and the Internet can also be outlets for puppy mills and backyard breeding. It's a tough call between "rescuing" a pup and perpetuating the puppy mill with your soft heart and dollars. Follow your instincts.

VETTING THE CANDIDATE

When choosing a dog that is compatible with all the variables of the "trail environment," you want to be able to screen the candidates as early as possible. Sitting in a room observing littermates and interacting with a pup can help you sort the bold from the shy, the dominant from the subordinate, and the independent from the responsive. Bloodline heredity and a thorough veterinary examination will give you a lot of tangible information about a dog's present and future physical condition.

Experts believe that a puppy's experiences during his first twelve weeks of life influence his potential to develop into a well-adjusted adult dog. Between sufficient time with their mother and littermates and exposure to humans and household activity, a responsible breeder will give pups a head start toward healthy social skills.

Educating yourself about the developmental stages and dogs' natural instincts can help you cope with and correct some behavioral problems if and when they surface.

THE MORE THE MERRIER VS. DOUBLE THE TROUBLE

Two puppies are twice as cute and entertaining but double the trouble. Yes, they will keep each other company. However, they will be partners in crime, bonding to each other rather than to you, which will make them much less responsive to training.

On the other hand, bringing a second dog into the household when the first is an adult (at least two years old) and well trained can be a lot of fun at home and on the trail. Dogs are pack animals. Even the presence of a pet of a different species can alleviate the solo dog's loneliness and boredom (the right cat often makes for a compatible companion).

Even with a pet companion, a dog should not be left at home for more than a four-hour stretch without human contact and access to a safe outdoor area.

Chapter Three

From the Whelping Box to the Trail (Bonding and Training)

Bonding is the loyalty, trust, and cooperation between you and your dog. A solid bond is crucial to successful training and fosters reliability on the trail. Bonding makes dogs more prone to please and therefore more likely to respond to commands.

SOCIALIZATION STAGES

Although there can be variations by breed and individuals, it is generally accepted that most puppies need to be with their mother and littermates until about eight weeks of age. The learning that occurs between mother and pup is one of the building blocks for a well-adjusted dog.

Puppies that engage in regular interactive play are smarter and settle easily in their slot in the pecking order because they have had plenty of opportunities to practice their social and communication skills. Dogs that are removed from the litter too young or are isolated from other dogs during this phase can later display excessive timidity or unprovoked aggression around other dogs.

Six to eight weeks is the peak age for human attachments. Pups need to be frequently handled by humans at this time. Introducing pups to new experiences during this phase—including the hum of daily household activity and basic training—will make future training easier.

Some dog breeds are more sensitive to "negative" imprinting if they are exposed to too much stimuli or encounter an unpleasant experience at a young age. Being overwhelmed by overly enthusiastic bigger dogs can cause a pup to retreat and become timid around other dogs rather than sociable. Don't put a pup in the lake or in a wave because you think he should learn how to swim. That can be a sure way to give him an aversion to water, including baths.

BONDING

After six to eight weeks of age, bonding occurs through consistent pleasurable interaction, including physical touch (from petting to massaging), feeding, walking, playing, training, and positive reinforcement of desired behavior through rewards (verbal praise, stroking, and treats). The more timid the dog, the more time, patience, and constant reassurance will be required to nurture it to some state of trust.

A dog regularly isolated in the yard, kennel, or a separate room can feel ostracized. Dogs need to be integrated into the daily activities of their human "pack" as much as possible. Hiking and backpacking excursions provide wonderful opportunities for quality bonding time.

Dog-friendly beaches are a great place for dogs to socialize and learn their place in the natural pecking order.

Play

Play is natural and essential to dogs. A dog's first bonding experience and lessons in social behavior come through play with her littermates. Pups thrive on play physically and mentally. In addition to being a good bonding tool, play promotes social skills, agility, and resourcefulness. A hike can be a shared playtime between you and your dog.

Experts warn against engaging in play-fighting with your dog during the socialization period, when you could be reinforcing dominance traits that could develop into aggression problems later.

Dogs raised as the "only dog" in the family benefit from play dates with other dogs to develop into well-adjusted animals.

Let the Games Begin

There are many games, activities, workshops, and sports designed to use dogs' natural abilities and instinct to help them develop confidence, stimulate their minds, burn calories, and reinforce the human/ canine bond. These activities do not have to be "competitive." From Frisbees and balls to agility and nose-work classes, these activities can just be a "fun" way to keep your dog fit, alert, and entertained off the trail. Nose work is one of the newest sports. Dogs' instinct to hunt or their love of toys is used to inspire them to locate a "target" scent or odor.

Food

Food is another way to a dog's heart. Dogs bond more readily to a hand that feeds them. In the case of a shy dog, begin by hand-feeding a few bites before putting the food bowl down. Dogs are always enthusiastic about the humans who give them treats and throw tennis balls.

Hand-feeding helps shy dogs build trust.

TRAINING TOTO

There are cultures where it is accepted for dogs to roam all day and come home for dinner and a bed. But in our society, with an ever-increasing number of dogs in closer urban quarters, managing dog behavior is also about respecting other people's space. This also applies to the hiking trails, where there are an increasing number of people with dogs who want to escape to nature on weekends and holidays.

On one hand, it's wonderful to see more people embracing the outdoors in the company of their dogs. But more trail users also means more pressure on the environment, wildlife habitat, and each other. Not everyone likes dogs, and not every hiker and backpacker is in favor of sharing the trail with dogs. Hikers and backpackers with dogs carry an extra responsibility. They can either represent a group that should have even more limited access to public lands or be ambassadors for the responsible dog owners who demonstrate good stewardship of the land. A well-behaved dog with obedience training promotes positive PR.

One of the gratifying aspects of obedience classes and hiking is that they complement each other. The drills prepare your dog, and the trail becomes a most enjoyable arena to practice and reinforce the classroom lessons. Obedience is especially important for a hiking dog because the nuisance and hazards of a few uncontrolled dogs can result in all dogs being banned from the trail.

Once you step out of your yard and onto the trail, everything your dog is and isn't reflects on you and impacts other people, animals, and the surrounding environment. Basic obedience skills are essential on the trail.

> **Your Dog's Trail ABCs**
>
> Appropriate behavior around everyone on the trail.
>
> Basic repertoire of verbal and/or hand signal commands, including sit, down, stay, and come.
>
> Controls his impulses and responds to commands (verbal or hand signals) in spite of the distracting sights, sounds, and smells of the trail.

Good Manners and Lifesavers

Use the word *off* when training your dog not to jump on people or dance on furniture. *Down* should be used strictly for lying down. It is unrealistic to expect an exuberant pup to respond to the *down* command under highly excitable circumstances. The best you can expect is for your dog to learn to display her excitement with all four paws touching the ground and stay "off." That drill, repeated over time, will prove to be one of your most challenging and rewarding accomplishments. Consistency and follow-through in your drills, reinforced by praise and food reward, are essential.

Teach your dog that when you say *stay* or *wait* when opening the car door, he should remain in the open vehicle until his leash is on and you've given the command that it's *okay* to jump out. (Leashing your dog before you open the door is a safe habit.)

Making a habit of having your dog sit and stay before a treat, coming in the house, stepping out of the house, or eating his food is a good "impulse" control exercise.

Training Options

There are several good training books available in the library, bookstores, pet supply stores, and online. The two main advantages of training your dog yourself are control of the training schedule and the minimal cost.

Having said that, it's more likely that novice dog owners intending to train their dog on their own with the help of a book will experience frustration, confuse their dog, create more bad habits than good ones, and inflict unnecessary stress on themselves and the dog while straining the relationship that had the potential of being the best one you could ever dream of.

The time and money invested in a puppy class followed by at least basic obedience in a group environment will give you invaluable rewards. Besides being introduced to basic commands, your pup will learn to walk on a loose leash.

Puppy classes and beginner's obedience classes are as much about "training" people as they are about "molding" your dog's behavior. This is where a qualified instructor teaches you to read your dog and give positive, clear messages to elicit the desired behaviors before you fall into the trap of having your dog "train" you or worse—having your murky communication foster a chaotic dysfunctional relationship that makes both dog and owner miserable.

Take the time to audit a couple of classes (a puppy class and a beginner's obedience class). It is amazing what you can learn about yourself just observing the dynamics between other owners and their dog. You will become an instant expert, picking out the dog owners who "get it." Notice how a qualified, intuitive trainer giving clear, confident, consistently positive verbal messages and physical cues can make a dog do what he wants. As a hiker and a backpacker, you want a positive relationship with your dog devoid of the negative emotional reactions and power struggles that are sure to undermine the team spirit necessary on the trail.

A good puppy class will teach you how to mold your pup's responsiveness to basic commands using fun drills and food rewards.

That's what a live class can do that a book cannot. Group classes also expose dogs to more stimuli and distractions, which help with socialization and impulse control. Dog owners are given exercises to practice between classes, and class is a place to come back to and measure progress. Beginner obedience classes also incorporate hand signals, which can be a valuable skill on the trail.

Group class schedules are available through kennel clubs, pet supply stores, and animal shelters.

The old adage that the dog owner is the "master" and dogs need to be "dominated" is archaic and thankfully passé as a basis for training. A good class emphasizes positive, reward-based techniques. Dogs should respond to a command with enthusiastic immediacy, not cowering compliance. You and your dog are a "pack" (a family of two or more), and you are the pack "leader" the dog learns to trust because you set the course with aplomb and consistency.

Puppies wear soft collars in class. Instructors will teach dog owners how to use choke-chain training collars appropriately on more mature dogs for obedience-training sessions only. These are *never* to be used as regular collars.

A qualified trainer can help you work with and around your dog's natural instincts and breed characteristics so that traits like dominance, guarding and chasing instincts, independence, hyper-alertness, or roaming do not become problems. A trainer can also

A structured group obedience class teaches your dog commands needed on the trail while learning to focus and ignore distractions.

instruct you in the appropriate use of tools such as the different types of head halters and no-pull harnesses, which are effective and humane, to teach your dog to walk on a loose leash.

Additional private sessions can be effective with adult dogs that require more one-on-one attention.

How Soon Should You Start Training Your Dog?

Dogs are not admitted to puppy classes until they are between ten and sixteen weeks, when they will have had at least their first two DHLP-P (distemper/parvo) vaccinations (by about ten to twelve weeks) or permission from their veterinarian. You should start working with your puppy on your own before that.

Basic training should start from the time the pup is born. Puppies that are handled by human hands earlier on bond more easily and accept human touch more readily. Practice calling your puppy enthusiastically to come and reward him with praise, petting, and a treat. This is the first step in many months of work toward every dog owner's ultimate goal: a reliable recall off-leash. *Never* use your dog's name to reprimand, punish, or administer anything she views as unpleasant. The more pleasant the experience, the more reason to come quickly.

Chapter Four

Training Tips and Tools

In the natural world, canines get their sense of security from pack order. The social order is essential to survival. It determines who breeds, leads, cares for the young, and guards, and who eats when. It's instinctive in your dog, and he will be more responsive, calmer, happier, and better integrated into the family if his position in the pack is reaffirmed. Every pack needs an alpha, a leader but not a bully. You should be that leader.

THE IMPORTANCE OF BEING CONSISTENT

Inconsistency breeds unpredictability. Rules and routines should be the same on the trail as they are at home. *No* should mean *no* anywhere. You don't want your dog testing you on the trail, where a rebellious act could put her life at risk or jeopardize someone else's safety.

>> Do reward your dog with a pat or a treat when he responds to a command.
>> Don't use your dog's name in a reprimand or call your dog to "come" to give him a reprimand. His name and the word *come* should be strictly associated with positive, pleasurable experiences.

POTTY-TRAINING TIPS FOR THE TRAIL

Conditioning your dog to relieve himself on command on-leash is a valuable habit on the way to the trailhead or anytime you may need to monitor where your dog relieves himself during the hike.

Begin at home by taking your dog outside on a leash at routine elimination times to the designated area. Use a short command phrase like "go potty," "hurry up," "get busy," or any comfortable expression (English or foreign language). Use the expression as your dog relieves himself, avoiding an overzealous tone that could distract him from business. Reward your dog with a pat, enthusiastic praise, and a treat.

Puppies have small bladders. They should be taken out when they wake up, right after play, about fifteen minutes after eating or drinking, before bedtime, and about every couple hours throughout the day when they are awake until they are about four months old.

CRATE—THE SAFE PRACTICAL PORTABLE DEN

Besides being useful for housebreaking (dogs don't soil their den unless unable to hold their bladder) and keeping pup safe when not under immediate supervision, proper crate training can apply to many situations, including being outdoors. Associating a crate with a cozy den becomes a safe way to travel to the trailhead. It is also a portable den where one dog can

Introduce your puppy to the crate as his safe, cozy space as early as possible.

feel content and secure in unfamiliar surroundings (campground, cabin, hotel room). Crate training can also make crating at the groomer's, veterinarian's, or boarding kennel less stressful.

The crate should be large enough for your dog to sit, stand, and move around comfortably with space for washable bedding, toys, food, and water dish.

To create a positive association for your dog:

1. Keep the crate where your dog feels part of the family activity.

2. Encourage your dog to investigate the crate with the door open after a good romp and

opportunity to relieve himself. Place toys and treats in the crate, and give him an affectionate rub when he is in the crate.

3. Feed all meals in the crate with the door open.

4. Close the crate door for a short while to gradually increase his time there. Limit crate time to two hours for pups under four months and no more than four hours for adult dogs, except at night. On the road, take crate breaks every two hours at any age.

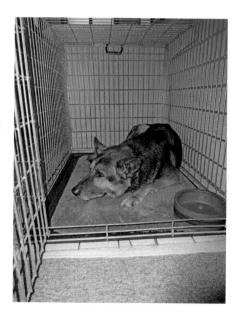

With patient positive training, even adult dogs can be conditioned to think of their crate as their favorite resting place.

GETTING TO THE TRAIL SAFELY

Ideally, your vehicle should be large enough to accommodate a dog crate or a dog barrier so that both dog and passengers are safe and comfortable. Dogs bouncing in the bed of a pickup truck are at risk of serious injury.

>> Provide adequate ventilation and shade from sun. In the summertime, cracking the window is *never* enough, even on a cloudy day.

>> Offer your dog water at every stop.

>> Train your dog to wait or stay in the crate or in the vehicle until you leash and invite him out with a command like *okay* or *hop out*. These can be lifesaving communication cues.

All Aboard

Initially, the vehicle should be stationary in the garage or driveway. The first few times, just turn on the engine and sit for a while. Next is a short drive down the street with a stop for a walk or a play session to promote the positive association with the car ride. Getting in the car only for veterinarian visits is a sure way to sabotage your road-training efforts.

Once you feel confident that your dog is comfortable riding in the car, take her with you around town: Stop at the park for a walk or even stroll through your local pet supply store for a biscuit. Drive smoothly, avoid winding roads, and gradually increase the length of the drives between routine stops.

Factor in frequent stops for stretching and sniffing when planning the drive time to the trailhead. Offer your dog water at every stop.

Motion Sickness

Dogs prone to motion sickness should not be fed on the morning of the drive; instead, feed them an hour after arrival or when they seem recovered from the stress of the drive. Food and hyperventilation can be an uncomfortable-to-dangerous combination, especially for large breeds with a predisposition to bloating. (See Chapter Seven under "Food/Exercise Risks.") Consult your veterinarian about the appropriate use of Dramamine to treat motion sickness and certain antihistamines for their calming effects, as opposed to medications that sedate.

Cool Ride

Make your dog more comfortable during a hot drive to and from the trailhead by covering his bedding with a wet towel or placing soft ice packs under a towel. Water-absorbent crate mats are available at pet supply stores, through mail-order catalogs, and online. Never leave your pet unattended in a vehicle for more than a very few minutes, and take a moment to slip a foldable sun-reflecting shield inside your windshield any time you park the car with your dog in it. It takes only a few minutes for your car to become a deadly oven, even with windows cracked.

BARKING

Barking is a form of communication, and dog talk comes in different tones, from the histrionic incessant barks of fear and alarm to the lonesome dog's plea for company. Some alert breeds are just naturally more vocal and feel it is their job to "keep watch" and "alert" their owners of anyone or anything they consider an intruder.

A barking dog at home is annoying, but in nature it is an unwelcome intrusion. If your dog is a chronic barker, identify the triggers and consult a qualified dog trainer for tips to correct the habit before you inadvertently reinforce the behavior.

A citronella spray anti-bark collar is one tool. Barking triggers the release of a burst of lemon-scented spray under your dog's nose. The unpleasant and startling citrus spray eliminates barking with most dogs. (Collars and refills are available from some veterinarians, trainers, pet stores, mail-order catalogs, and online.)

Shock collars and remote "pressure" collars are effective only if properly used. They can be inhumane and harmful to your dog's throat and windpipe if you don't know what you're doing. Dogs have suffered severe burns all the way to their trachea with shock collars, and too much repetitive pressure on the throat can lead to other problems requiring invasive and expensive surgery.

Chapter Five

Fit for the Trail

Preparing your dog for hiking is like coaching an athlete for an Olympic decathlon. You must get her in good physical condition (muscular and cardiovascular) to enjoy the hike safely. Certain parts of your dog's body will require special care and attention before hiking to prevent injury or discomfort. Mental conditioning includes familiarizing her with hiking equipment and the trail environment.

PRE-HIKE CARE

Dewclaws: All dogs are born with front dewclaws, and many have rear dewclaws. This fifth digit on the inside of the leg is prone to tearing and ideally should

Properly trimmed nails make for comfortable paws and good traction on the trail.

Booties come in different styles and materials. Try them on your dog for the best fit and function.

be removed by a veterinarian within a few days after birth. Otherwise, have this surgery done when your dog is spayed or neutered.

Nails: Nails should be comfortably short without sacrificing traction. Even dogs that are active enough outdoors to keep their nails naturally worn need to have the nail on the dewclaw trimmed. Consult a groomer or your veterinarian on using dog nail clippers and a nail file for maintenance between clips.

Feet: Dog footpads get toughened to a light sandpaper texture by regular and gradually extended walks and runs on rough and varied surfaces. Booties should be worn to alleviate tenderness and protect footpads from cuts on ice and sharp rocks.

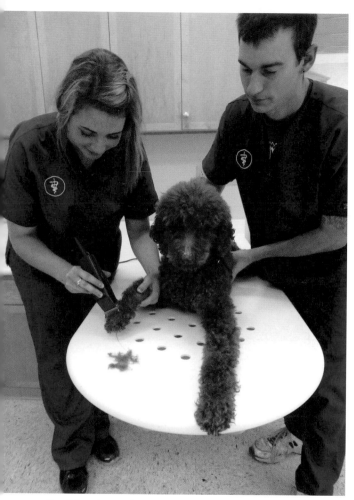

Pre-hike trims make grooming easier on the trail.

Grooming: Long coats should be trimmed (not shaved), particularly under the belly and behind the legs during the summer. Trimming hair between the toes prevents foxtails (invasive grasses found primarily in the western United States) from going undetected while they burrow, puncture, and infect and prevents the formation of icicles around the pads, decreasing the chance of frostbite.

Spaying and neutering: Your dog will be just as smart, loving, and trim after he or she is altered. Altering does not make dogs fat—too much food and too little exercise do. Besides the social and medical benefits of altering—reduced incidence of mammary gland cancer in females and prostate cancer in males—a decreased sexual drive will make your pet less apt to roam or tangle with other dogs. The trail advantage of neutering is a male dog that is more congenial and less preoccupied with competition around other males.

Vaccinations: Your dog should be current on all vaccinations (DHLP-P, rabies, and a vaccination against Lyme disease are advisable). The veterinary community's thinking on annual vaccines has evolved over the last few years, and many veterinarians now customize vaccine regimens to the individual dog, taking into account age and lifestyle. Discuss these changes with your veterinarian. Also ask him or her about the recent vaccine against rattlesnake venom.

Heartworm: Mosquitoes carry this parasite. Consult your veterinarian about preventive medication.

West Nile virus: Mosquitoes carry this virus. At this time there have been no reports of noticeable symptoms or fatal infections in canines. No vaccine or specific treatment exists.

Fleas and ticks: Dogs can be infected with tapeworms when they ingest fleas that are carriers of tapeworm eggs. Some types of ticks are also carriers of disease (see Chapter Nine). Flea and tick products are abundant on the market today. Consult your veterinarian on the best treatment for your dog.

BUILDING CONFIDENCE

Exposure to the trail environment at an early age (preferably before twelve weeks) will help build your dog's confidence. Dogs get comfortable with sounds, sights, and experiences by early and constant exposure as pups (ideally before sixteen weeks old). Beyond four months of age, new experiences are met with a degree of natural apprehension and caution.

If your dog has already developed a fear of certain situations, you will need to recondition her by introducing the threatening stimuli gradually in small doses. This is typical of the more primitive breeds and hybrids, whose acute survival instincts prevent them from taking the new and unusual in stride.

On the other hand, this environmental hyperawareness can be an asset on the trail. Such a dog may sense and communicate real dangers to you before you even see, hear, or feel the hint of a threat. He may be the one to smell or see the bear, hear the landslide, or feel a precarious situation developing.

Trail Sights

Let your dog get used to seeing backpacks, walking sticks, tents, and other hiking equipment around the house. Simulate trail circumstances by having friends with hats, backpacks, walking sticks, and fishing rods stroll around the yard or come around the corner while you are on a walk with your dog. There may be horses, pack stock, and cyclists on the trail, so introduce your dog to these ahead of time.

BUILDING STAMINA

Puppies Eight to Sixteen Weeks Old

Even a backyard can be full of adventures and exploration possibilities for a pup. It's a good idea to introduce your pup to the natural hiking setting as early as possible, but you must be sensible about her vulnerability to infectious diseases. Puppies get their initial immunity from their mother's milk, but they need protection through inoculation after they stop nursing.

Make your backyard your dog's nature playground until he has had all the immunization shots needed to step out on the trail.

By twelve weeks your puppy should have had the first of three DHLP-P vaccinations. Although it may be reasonably safe to socialize and romp around other pups on the same vaccination schedule, hold off on the great outdoors until she has had her final series of DHLP-P and rabies vaccination (four to six months). Try to take her to a park, beach, or neighborhood trail for exercise and sensory stimulation (twenty- to thirty-minute sessions) in addition to playtime and at least two leash walks daily. Use good sense, and don't expose your pup to strange dogs or other animals until she has been vaccinated against rabies.

Puppies Four to Six Months Old

By now your puppy should be fully immunized and can safely venture away from the grassy green belts of civilization and closer to nature. Fields, meadows, or nearby forested trails will be more stimulating for your pup, although the distractions will make training more challenging for both of you.

Use a long rope or expandable leash (20 to 30 feet) so your pup can romp and explore under controlled conditions. Practice *sit, stay, down,* and *come* at the end of the rope several times.

Let him off in a safe area of the trail and practice calling him enthusiastically during these pre-hike drills, rewarding him with a "good dog," a pat, and treats. Always use verbal praise and a pat, and when the desired behavior becomes consistent, use food rewards only some of the time.

Don't reward or coddle if your dog doesn't perform the desired behavior. That just reinforces the wrong behavior, confuses the dog, and frustrates the owner, creating a cycle of negativity. The owner is to blame, not the dog.

Tell your dog to "go play," and do not call him unless you have eye contact or know you have his attention. He does not hear you when he is absorbed smelling, listening, or digging for creatures. Do not compete and set yourselves up for failure.

Never call him to you for a reprimand, no matter how frustrated you may be with his behavior.

These introductory training excursions (thirty minutes to one hour) will leave an overactive puppy calm and sleepy for his indoor life. Remember that during the first several months (six for small dogs, nine to twelve for larger dogs), most of the dog's energy is going into the growth of his young body. Do not stress the healthy development of your dog's muscles and bones with long distances and hills. With giant breeds, until twelve to eighteen months, keep the excursions short (under an hour) and on mostly flat terrain.

Take frequent rest stops and water breaks. In warm weather, stop every twenty minutes for your puppy to rest and drink water.

Neither training nor the excursions themselves should be endurance events for the dog to puff up the owner's ego. None of it is about proving how "tough" anyone is. Hiking and backpacking with your dog is about mutual enjoyment of the greatest play-ground on earth.

Adult Dogs

Gradual conditioning principles also apply to adult dogs that are just being introduced to the fun of hiking. If your dog's arena of physical activity has been primarily in the yard, begin by planning a walking route that allows you to be out thirty minutes twice daily (morning and evening). Consult your physician and your veterinarian before making any changes to your and your dog's physical activity level.

TRAINING REGIMEN

Following is an example of a reasonable five-week training regimen to help new hikers and backpackers (dogs in their prime, generally ages two through seven) get muscles, cardio, and paw pads ready for the trail. The length and frequency can be adjusted based on the owner's and dog's lifestyle, baseline activity level, and health condition.

Week 1
Morning and Evening (approx. 1 mile 2x daily)
15 minutes sniff and stroll (warm-up)
10 minutes brisk walk (cardiovascular workout)
5 minutes sniff and stroll (cooldown)

Week 2
Morning and Evening (approx. 1–1.5 miles 2x daily)
15 minutes sniff and stroll (warm-up)
15–20 minutes brisk walk (cardiovascular workout)
5 minutes sniff and stroll (cooldown)

Week 3
Morning and Evening (approx. 2 miles 2x daily)
15 minutes sniff and stroll (warm-up)
20–30 minutes brisk walk (cardiovascular workout)
5 minutes sniff and stroll (cooldown)

Weeks 4 and 5
Morning and Evening (approx. 3 miles 2x daily)
15 minutes sniff and stroll (warm-up)
30–45 minutes brisk walk (cardiovascular workout)
10 minutes sniff and stroll (cooldown)

By Week 3, owner and dog should be starting to wear their packs on the walks, gradually increasing the weight in the pack to what each will be comfortably expected to carry on a day hike or the first backpack overnight. Remember the weight guidelines for the dog's pack (see Chapter Seven). By now you should gradually be incorporating hills and stairs to strengthen muscles and simulate the exertion of the backcountry's ups and downs.

By Week 5, the fitter team should plan on a longer weekend walk (5 to 6 miles) focusing on distance, not speed, to get a sense of your progress and what you can comfortably plan on for your first day hike or overnight. Your dog's pads will begin to roughen. Remember that if you have been walking on paved

Training for the trail can begin with brisk neighborhood walks.

Stairs are a great cardio training ground for the changing elevations of the trail.

surfaces, dirt hiking trails, rockier terrain, and elevation changes will make the going slower and more strenuous. Expect some feedback from your feet and legs at the end of the day.

Use the Week 5 regimen as a guideline for maintaining your dog's conditioning between hikes.

Ideally, your dog should be getting at least two hours of outdoor exercise daily, including walks and off-leash playtime. If you live near a dog-friendly beach, this is an ideal place for play and socialization. The grit of the sand is good pad conditioning. Make sure your dog always has drinking water, shade, and rest as needed.

During summer, shade from trees or cooling off in surface water helps dogs regulate their body temperature. If your dog decides to lounge in a mud puddle, let her. A dirty dog is the least of your worries.

Sprinting on the beach is a good cardio workout for you and your dog, while the sand friction helps toughen his pads.

PACE SETTER

To get a baseline on your stride and pace, time yourself walking around the local high school track with your dog on leash. (Tracks are generally 0.25 mile per lap.) Also take into account rest, refueling (water and snacks), and photo stops, along with terrain, elevation, and steepness, when estimating the time it will take to complete a hike.

In the mountains, for every 1,000 feet of elevation gain, add the time it takes you to hike 1 mile to calculate the total time of the hike.

Hiking downhill is not twice as fast as hiking uphill. It takes about three-quarters of the time to hike the same distance downhill.

HEALTH CONSIDERATIONS

Consult your veterinarian to help evaluate your dog's health and discuss under what conditions hiking would be beneficial.

This is not to say that if your dog is older, overweight, or has a medical condition she cannot hike. But if common sense precludes a human couch potato from sprinting a mile or driving to 8,000 feet for a 5-mile hike, the same applies to a dog who divides his time between the yard and his dog bed.

Keep it safe and fun!

Chapter Six

Planning the Adventure (When and Where)

Every hike shares routine preparations, but some destinations require more specific planning. In addition, the coast, mountains, desert, and forest offer different sources of enjoyment in different seasons as well as challenges that can affect your dog.

Desert hikes require extra attention to dehydration. Offer your dog water more frequently and in the shade when available.

SEASONAL CONSIDERATIONS

SUMMER heat can be taxing on your dog. The dry heat of the West, however, is more tolerable than the humidity of the South and East.

Minimizing Dehydration and Heat Stroke Risk

» Hike in the early morning or late afternoon.
» Carry at least 8 ounces of water per dog for each hour on the trail or 3 miles of trail.
» Rest in a shaded area during the intensity of midday.
» Make frequent stops, and offer your dog water.
» Let your dog take a plunge in the lake or lie belly-down in a stream or mud puddle to cool down.

WINTER conditions will affect your dog's feet, endurance, and body warmth. Crusty snow can chafe and cut your dog's pads, and walking in deep snow is very taxing and can put a short-haired dog at risk of hypothermia.

Protect your Dog from Cold and Extra Exertion

» Carry booties for icy conditions, and use them on dogs not accustomed to winter weather. Take a couple extras as replacements for any lost in the snow. Keeping your dog on-leash while he is in booties makes it easier to know when to adjust them or to retrieve any that slip off. (See Chapter Seven for bootie tips.)

Don't pass a stream without letting your dog cool down.

- » Clothing on dogs should be about function, not fashion. Consider a wool or polypropylene sweater for a short-haired dog or down for a dog with no undercoat.
- » Encourage your dog to walk behind you in your tracks. It is less strenuous.
- » Take a small sled or snow disk with an insulated foam pad so your dog can rest off the frozen ground.
- » Unless your dog is a northern breed that thrives in cold and snow, keep your outings shorter in winter, and carry snacks like liver or jerky treats and warm drinking water.

Even dogs accustomed to snow can get abraded paws. Check their feet for chafing, and carry booties as a backup.

SPRING, in some parts of the country, means heavy rain, mosquitoes, fleas, ticks, and a new crop of poison oak and poison ivy. Be informed about regional seasonal conditions and the potential impact on your dog's comfort on the trail. See Chapter Nine to find out about trail nuisances so you can be prepared to address them.

FALL announces hunting season in many parts of the backcountry. Check the hunting regulations and dates for the hiking area you have in mind. Most important, you and your dog should wear bright colors when hiking anywhere in the fall. Orange hunting vests are available for dogs, and colorful harnesses and bandannas are a good idea. When in doubt about hunting, keep your dog on a leash on forested trails.

Remember that fall brings shorter daylight hours. Adjust the length of your hikes so you do not risk getting stranded on the trail in the dark unprepared.

KNOW WHAT TO EXPECT

Always get information ahead of time about the area where you want to hike.

Determine which agency regulates the area (national, state, regional, or other). Call ahead or visit the relevant website for the most up-to-date rules and restrictions on dogs on the trails. Is it "on-leash" or "voice control"?

Do you need a permit?

What wildlife is in the area? The region's fish and wildlife, park, or forest headquarters can give you a heads up about safety concerns for you and your dog. Keep your eyes open, and learn to identify tracks, scat, and concealed mountain lion kill sites. Keep your dog on a leash in questionable areas.

What is the weather pattern?

The high country is subject to more variable and extreme weather. Check the weather forecast and fire danger advisory at a ranger station.

Afternoon thunderstorms in the summer are common, and it is best to be below the timberline and off exposed ridges.

In the spring and fall, pay attention to sudden drops in temperature and clouds moving in announcing snowfall.

What are the trail conditions?

Advisories about fast water, high streams, and trail damage are commonly posted at a ranger station or visitor center. If nothing is posted, ask anyway. Always try to speak to someone who has recently hiked the trail, especially at the beginning of the season.

Where are we?

The USGS map with a scale of 1:24,000 (also known as 7.5-minute) is the standard for trail navigation. These maps contain information about forest headquarters, roads, trailheads and trails, picnic areas and campgrounds, glaciers and permanent snowfields, along with boundaries for parks, forests, and monuments. Their contour lines indicate elevation changes so you can determine how flat or hilly your route will be. Remember that each 1,000 feet of elevation gain is like hiking an extra mile.

USGS maps also indicate shady woodlands and sunny meadows and the location of rivers, lakes, or springs in case you need water.

Most smart phones and some tablets have a built-in GPS that displays your location even when you are outside cell or Wi-Fi range. The best apps allow you to download USGS maps into your device showing your location, speed, and direction. Dedicated GPS units usually have larger screens, along with longer battery life and more options.

The batteries in electronic devices can go dead. Devices cannot always pick up GPS satellite signals. The smart hiker carries a waterproof USGS map and a compass as a safety net. Be aware that maps do not always reflect the most up-to-date trail info, such as a closure or rerouting. Confirm the existence, location, and condition of the trail with a ranger. Whatever your navigation system, practice around your neighborhood and study the map ahead of time. Plan the most comfortable route for your dog based on season and terrain.

Who knows where you are?

Leave a copy of your itinerary with a friend or family member, and check in when you return.

Chapter Seven

Pack It Up and Move It Out

You and your dog can smell the trail, and you can't wait to feel the dirt under your boots and paws.

GEARING UP FOR A DAY HIKE

There are certain items necessary to make your day hikes safe and more enjoyable with your dog. The following describes gear options that can further increase your safety and that of your dog and enhance your hiking experience. Many of the day hike equipment items are essential building blocks to a successful backpacking excursion.

Collars and Harnesses

Either a collar or harness is suitable, but a colorful harness makes your dog more visible and identifies him as domestic. For dogs of intimidating size or appearance, a colorful harness emphasizes their pet status. A harness is a safer restraint (a collar could slip off or choke the animal) if your dog were ever in a predicament requiring you to pull him out of water or hoist him up a hillside.

Harnesses reduce the risk of neck injury or suffocation from a snag or tangle in brush or a branch. With an adult dog that insists on pulling you along, the harness will give you more control and prevent damage to his neck and throat.

Never use a choke-chain training collar as a permanent collar. It can be deadly. Strangulation has occurred when another dog's jaw has gotten twisted in the choke collar during rambunctious play. A dog can snag a choke collar on a low branch while running through the brush or slip and fall off a boulder, hanging himself at the end of a leash and choke collar.

Material: Although leather is the most durable, nylon collars and harnesses are available in vibrant colors, are usually adjustable, and dry more quickly. Plastic collars in bright colors are also practical for wet

A harness allows for a quick grab of your dog in an emergency, and a colorful harness makes him more visible on the trail.

situations. Your dog is less likely to lose a collar or harness with a plastic snap-in clasp than a metal buckle when he's running, swimming, and jostling about.

Fit: You should be able to easily slip your flat hand under the collar and rotate the collar but not slip it over the dog's head. A puppy will need to be fitted with a new collar a few times as he grows. Harnesses need to fit loosely enough to allow full expansion of the chest and a free stride.

Identification Tags

Microchipping a dog is a great idea but won't do you any good in the wilderness, where there are no veterinarian offices or animal shelters equipped to read the chip. On the trail a tag is the most obvious way to reunite a lost dog and its owner. The tag should include the dog's name and home phone with area code if you do not have a cell phone number.

The sight, smell, or sound of another animal could lure your dog away, and thunder or gunshots could startle your dog and cause her to run off. You want to facilitate a reunion. If another person gets close enough to your dog to see the tag, the first thing he or she will look for is a name. Calling the dog by its name will establish some communication and trust. The telephone number allows the finder to leave a message on voicemail if you are out of cell reach.

Smart phone technology is being used to develop GPS devices that attach to the collar for tracking down lost pets. Check out ConsumerReports.org for a review of three such devices.

Temporary Identification
Your dog should also have a temporary identification tag when you are hiking out of town. The tag should have the date, location (campground, cabin, or trailhead name), and a telephone / cell phone number.

Securing the Tag
Loop rings are more secure than S rings for attaching tags. Small plastic luggage tags on a loop ring make inexpensive reusable temporary tags.

Leashes
A leash that will suffer the abuse of the trail (streams, rain, snow, and rocks) must be durable. Colorful nylon webbed leashes are light, dry quickly, and are easy to spot when you lay them down. You can inexpensively design your own leash by buying the webbed nylon by the foot at a mountaineering store and the clasp at a hardware store.

Traditional leather leashes stay the cleanest, last forever, and are recommended in obedience classes. Place a piece of colored tape or tie a strand of colored fabric to the handle to make finding the leash easier when it is on the ground.

Retractable leashes come in various lengths and weights to match the weight and size of the dog pulling at the other end. They offer a balance between control and freedom for urban settings. However, you don't want to get caught reeling your dog in around trees, people, or other dogs in an emergency situation.

Bandannas

A colorful bandanna around a dog's neck sends two important messages. It can say "cute," which helps make big dogs look less intimidating to other hikers. In the forest, a bright bandanna also says "domestic," which helps distinguish dogs from game during the hunting season.

Tie the bandanna on a colorful harness for maximum visibility. Little Gypsy had never been off–leash, and his gray-and-white-camouflage-colored coat made him blend with the trees when I first began to train him on recall off leash. I clipped a bright fluorescent pink leash to his red harness so that I could quickly locate him visually and take control if he wandered.

Reflective Vest

When hiking during hunting season, your dog should wear a bright, lightweight, reflective vest, designed for sporting dogs. This helps distinguish your dog from wildlife.

Booties

If your dog is only an occasional hiker that spends most of his time sauntering across the lawn at home, his pads may get tender after even just a couple of

Attaching a colorful leash to your dog's harness is a good way to keep visual track of him during recall drills on the trail.

miles. Booties can give relief to your dog's sore paws until his pads toughen, as well as prevent cuts from crusty or icy trail conditions.

Your dog should practice wearing booties in the house and on neighborhood walks. Booties are available in different paw sizes and materials. The new flexible rubber and biodegradable kinds are lightweight and handy as backups to the more specialized booties. You can purchase booties at pet supply and mountaineering stores, online, or through mail-order catalogs, and they are advertised in dog sledding magazines. It's best to purchase your first pair where you can try on different types and sizes to determine what style best conforms to your dog's paws.

Dog Packs

Most packs are designed to rest on the dog's back like a saddle with a pouch on each side. Packs are most appropriate for overnight trips and long day hikes, and should only be carried by fit medium-to-large adult dogs.

There's significantly more gear when you go overnight, and it's a good use of dog power to train a medium or large dog to assist by carrying her booties, first-aid kit, food, and treats or other accessories related to her needs. Packs come in different sizes and configurations and have become somewhat of a fashion statement. Small breeds with big-dog ambition can feel purposeful by carrying treats and a stash of waste bags in their packs.

Pack Fitting

Packs are sold at pet supply, outdoor recreation, and mountaineering stores, and through online specialty retailers and mail-order catalogs. They come in different sizes with adjustable straps. Your dog's comfort depends on a proper fit. Purchasing your packs at a local retailer enables you to try different styles on your dog and determine which design best conforms to your dog's body. The pack should feature breathable material, rounded corners, and padding for additional comfort.

The pack needs to sit on his shoulders between the base of the neck and short of the hips. There should be one strap that clips at the front of his chest and one or two belly straps to stabilize the pack. Straps should be tight enough to keep the pack in place but loose enough to allow full stride without chafing and comfortable expansion of the chest for breathing.

Pack Training

Packs are an opportunity to give fit adult dogs that weigh more than thirty-five pounds the sense of purpose so many thrive on. With patient proper training, these enthusiastic bundles of dog muscle power can learn to carry food and backpacking accessories.

It is important that loaded packs should only be carried by adult dogs that have reached full physical maturity. *The total weight on your dog's back should not exceed a quarter of its weight* (for example, a forty-pound dog should not carry more than ten pounds of evenly distributed weight).

Begin by placing a face cloth or small towel on your dog's back to introduce him to the feel of weight on his back. Leave the pack around the house near his bed or crate for a few days and in the car when you take him for a ride.

Feed him little treats while you try the pack on him (empty), and praise him for having the pack on. Take it off and repeat the exercise twice a day for about a week.

The next step is to put the pack on for going on a leash walk. Give him a treat while you are putting the pack on, and then put his leash on as you would on a regular walk.

Put the pack on your dog for short hikes with only treats in the pouches, so you can take the treats from his pack on snack breaks. The idea is to create

Let your dog get used to the feel of the empty pack before gradually increasing the evenly distributed load. The loaded pack should not weigh more than one-quarter of an adult dog's weight.

positive associations with the pack so that eventually the sight of the pack evokes an enthusiastic response from your dog.

Pack Loading

Don't estimate—weigh your dog. Stuff the pack with crumpled newspaper at first or a pair of empty plastic water bottles. Just like your shoulders, long hours with loads will make your dog's muscles sore.

Once he is accustomed to the pack and his endurance is built up, gradually increase the load by filling the water bottles to 10 percent of his weight, not to exceed one-quarter of his weight. If you use a pack only occasionally, keep the weight on the lighter side. The weight should be equal and evenly distributed to avoid interfering with your dog's balance. Incorporate pack training into your five-week training program (see Chapter Five).

Pack Safety

Keep your dog on-leash when he is wearing his pack. Packs can make balance awkward when negotiating narrow mountainside trails or crossing fast streams. Give him a break every hour or so by removing the pack so he enjoys the freedom you both came for by playing, swimming, and rolling around without risking injury to himself and damage to his pack and cargo.

Life Vest

Some dogs are stronger swimmers and more drawn to water than others, but a life vest keeps any dog safe if you are going to hike near rivers and lakes or if you have to cross high or fast-moving water. An elderly or tired dog is more at risk in the water during a hike than she would be playing at the beach.

Flashlight and Extra Batteries

You will be thankful for a flashlight—especially one that fits in a day pack—if you are still hiking after sunset. Many of the smaller flashlights now have very bright LED lighting.

You should fit your dog with a life vest for safer crossings of deep or fast-moving water.

Matches and Cigarette Lighter

Temperatures can drop quickly after the sun goes down. If you are lost or injured, a fire can help keep you warm until daylight or help arrives. Put matches and a strike strip in a pill bottle to protect them from the elements. Gas clicker lighters are lightweight and can be easier to use in inclement weather.

Lightweight Nylon Tarp

In an emergency, a tarp makes a lightweight shelter from sun, wind, and rain. Purchase a lightweight one at a local hardware or outdoor store.

Flyers for a Lost Dog

Carry a few photocopied flyers with your dog's photo, name, and a contact phone number. If the unfortunate happens, you can fill in a description of the area where your dog was lost and post flyers at the trailhead, campground, and ranger station and carry one to show to other hikers along the way.

Food

Dogs require a balanced diet made up of five essential nutrients: protein, fat, carbohydrates, minerals, and vitamins. Our food supply is not as wholesome as it once was, in part due to increased processing, additives, pesticides, and other manipulations. Dogs share our food supply, and their health is also affected by the quality control of what we feed them.

Human food (cooked poultry, meat, and rice) is tasty and freshest. Raw food diets for dogs have become more popular, and many breeders and owners are believers in the health benefits. Dry kibble remains the most lightweight, convenient staple for the trail and can easily be supplemented with healthy, nutritious human food to meet the protein and fat calorie needs of a hiking dog.

Read the ingredients and avoid brands with animal by-products and corn fillers. Choose a formula that matches your dog's age group and activity level, such as puppy growth, adult maintenance, high performance, and senior for less-active dogs.

If your dog has a medical condition or allergies that require a restricted diet, your veterinarian is the first source for advice. The breeder can also guide you in choosing appropriate food for your dog.

Chow Time

Puppies are generally fed three or four smaller meals per day. Just as smaller, more frequent meals are healthier for humans, adult dogs should be fed at least twice a day. Divide their total daily portion into two smaller meals (morning and evening). Exercising on a full stomach is uncomfortable because most of the body's blood supply is busy helping with digestion rather than supplying oxygen to the muscles and cardiovascular system.

It is not necessary to increase your dog's amount of food for a day hike. Instead, supplement his diet at snack breaks. Pack dog biscuits, jerky treats, and a pouch of semimoist food or extra dry kibble. Some dogs like carrots, apples, and melon pieces as much as any canine treat. (Remember that chocolate is toxic to dogs.)

In cold weather, bring higher-protein dog snacks. Look for real liver, turkey, chicken, or egg as the first ingredient, and avoid products with sugar and fillers.

Food/Exercise Risks

There are differing theories on the condition called gastric dilatation-volvulus complex (GDV), which involves bloating and stomach torsion. The most popular explanation suggests that strenuous exercise (jumping and running) after a large meal may compound the risks of the stomach twisting in the abdomen, blocking the flow or absorption of gastric material. Large breeds are especially prone to GDV, which can be fatal. Dividing daily portions into smaller, more frequent meals, preferably fed during rest periods on the trail or in camp, can help prevent GDV.

Plastic Resealable Bags

The airtight, self-sealing invention is in the top five essentials for the trail. These bags are great for carrying food, treats, medication, and first-aid necessities, and they can easily be converted into food and water bowls. Their "sealing" quality comes in handy for disposing of dog waste.

Water

Water is as essential to your dog as it is to you. Do not skimp on bringing water or count on finding it along the trail. Dehydration can result in sluggishness, kidney problems, and heat stroke. Both humans and dogs are vulnerable to dehydration in the heat and at high elevations.

Do not let your dog drink from standing water in puddles, ponds, lakes, or swimming holes in slow-moving creeks and rivers. That's where different forms of bacteria and algae breed, and small dogs and puppies have been known to get very ill and in some cases die from drinking contaminated water. Be especially wary of areas where cattle graze.

Make sure you take advantage of every freshwater source along the trail.

Both dogs and humans are susceptible to the intestinal parasite *Giardia lamblia,* which can cause cramping and diarrhea, leading to serious dehydration. Giardia can be present in all sources of untreated water.

How Much Water Do I Need?

Carry at least 8 ounces of water per dog per hour of hiking. Consider that an average walking pace on level ground is about 3 miles per hour. Fill plastic water bottles (three-quarters full) and place in the freezer the night before. Your dog will have a source of cool, fresh water as the ice melts along the way. Two frozen water bottles can also keep her cooler if you place one in each pouch of her dog pack.

Offer your dog water frequently (every half hour or more on hot days). It is easier to regulate hydration with regular small intakes of water.

Snow may keep your dog cool, but do not believe that a hot, thirsty dog will instinctively know to eat snow to quench her thirst. One hiker reported that her Southern California–born-and-raised dog was almost delirious from dehydration after she took him on a summer hike up a mountain where she thought the abundant snow would make up for the lack of water.

Bowls

Weight and encumbrances are the main concerns when packing for a hike. There are plenty of ways to create inexpensive doggie dinnerware on the trail. Paper or plastic picnic plates and bowls are lightweight and adequate for food and water. A plastic resealable bag can store the kibble and convert into a food dish or water bowl (hold the bag while your dog drinks from it). Pet supply stores, outdoor recreation stores, online pet supply retailers, and mail-order catalogs have numerous doggie gadgets for carrying and serving food and water on the trail, from canteens to collapsible bowls.

First-Aid Kit

Although you cannot prepare for all the mishaps, it is best to have a few first-aid items. See Appendix B for a first-aid kit checklist.

SLEEPOVERS IN NATURE

Backpacking with your dog requires some extra necessities and additional planning. You should incorporate your fully loaded backpack into the five-week training regimen by gradually increasing the weight in your own pack as well as your dog's over the course of the last two weeks of training.

The first backpacking trip should be as positive an experience as possible to leave you and pooch wanting more. If you and your dog are newcomers to backpacking, a close-by single overnight with a friend who is an experienced backpacker might ensure a

Camping is an opportunity for you and your dog to get comfortable with your gear and routine before setting out for the backcountry.

positive and safer initiation to the activity and be a confidence-building opportunity. Keep your distance from the trailhead to about 3 miles in case you need to beat a quick retreat.

Permits

Permits are generally obtained from ranger stations of the government agency that manages the land you wish to hike on (e.g., national or state park and forest, Bureau of Land Management). Permits are usually required for overnights in wilderness areas and in other heavily used recreation areas. In some places, registering or obtaining a permit can be required even for day hiking. In areas where use is strictly regulated, you may have to apply for a permit several months ahead of time.

Food

Make a list of the number of meals and snacks per hiking day for you and your dog. Package your dog's meals and snacks (preferably dry or semimoist) individually in resealable bags for convenience and to keep food smells from attracting bears.

You can safely supplement your dog's dry kibble with most human food you would bring for yourself, except sugar and chocolate (chocolate is toxic to dogs as well as cats). Plan to take one extra cup of human food per day to supplement your dog's dinner in camp. Pasta and rice are lightweight and easy to cook in camp and can be prepared creatively for extra taste and nutrition.

Meat eaters can add canned tuna, salmon, or chicken, as well as any freeze-dried meat sauce or soup mix. Either way, your dog will appreciate the added flavor to her kibble and will benefit from the energy fuel. (**Note:** Introduce her to new foods at home gradually before going on the trail.)

Cutting your dog's regular dog food with puppy food will add the extra protein and fat needed for the higher calorie-burning excursions. Begin mixing in small amounts of puppy food about three days before the hike so your dog's digestive system can adapt gradually.

Water

You need to take enough water for drinking (for you and the dog) and cooking. If you are sure of the availability of water, consider carrying less and boiling, filtering, or chemically treating the water in camp. There are several water purification systems available at outdoor recreation stores, but be aware that some dogs will not drink chemically treated water.

Bedding

For your dog, carry a piece of foam and a towel, which you can roll up with your sleeping bag. Or try a lightweight dog bedroll, designed to be cuddly on one side and durable on the side in contact with the ground. Dog bedrolls are available at pet supply stores, through mail-order catalogs, and online.

If you choose to sleep under the stars, make sure your dog is staked on a line (6-foot radius from his stake or tree) short enough to keep him away from the campfire but long enough to allow him to have physical contact with you. Physical contact gives your dog the security that will help keep him quieter if the sounds of the dark outdoors are new to him. It enables you to hush him at the first hint of a growl, keeps him warmer on cold nights, and lets you know when he's on alert.

12 Tips for Camp Housekeeping

Evening

1. Pick your campsite in daylight, taking into account exposure, water, mosquitoes, and your dog's comfort.

2. Put your dog on her tie-out line, where she can curl up to rest, and give her water while you set up camp (sleeping and cooking quarters). Keep her water bowl full and within easy reach but out of the "step and spill" zone.

3. Get enough water to boil or filter for cooking dinner and breakfast, and enough drinking water for you and pooch for the evening and following trail day (8 ounces per mile per dog).

4. Prepare dinner for you and pooch.

5. Wash the dishes and burn or seal garbage in plastic bags for pack-out to remove any food smells from camp.

6. Use the bear-proof metal food storage bins whenever provided, and consider buying your own small bear-proof canisters for your aromatic goods.

7. Walk your dog before bedtime, take one last walk around to tidy up camp from any bear-magnet residuals left over, like food wrappers.

8. Snuggle up for the night.

Morning

9. Walk your dog and clean up any of her waste.

10. Share a hot breakfast with her (instant hot cereal or scrambled eggs over her kibble, with a hot drink for you and warm water for her).

Plan to make camp in daylight. It's safer and allows you and your dog time to kick back and savor the destination after all the planning and training to get there.

11. Clean up.
12. Pack up, leaving your campsite cleaner than you found it.

Stay with Your Dog

Three reasons why your dog should be attended in camp at all times:

1. He would be vulnerable to wild predators if left alone.
2. He might suffer stress from being separated from you in unfamiliar surroundings.
3. He might ruin the wilderness experience for other campers if he expresses his separation anxiety through barking, whining, and howling. Do not forget that separation anxiety could also bring on a chewing rampage that might leave you with a shredded tent, sleeping bag, or backpack.

Chapter Eight

Sharing the Trail (Etiquette and Safety)

Trail etiquette boils down to good dog manners and reliability of that behavior. Even in areas where a leash is not mandatory, control is. Dogs can be shot for harassing livestock and wildlife. Trail etiquette is especially important for maintaining good relations between those with and without dogs.

Keeping your dog on a leash when hiking near livestock is safer for your dog and the livestock.

MINIMIZE DOG–DOG CONFLICTS

At one time or another, your dog may be a partner in a dominance dance with another dog. This occurs more frequently between males, especially intact males that reek of testosterone. Dogs well versed in pack hierarchy know to stay out of an alpha dog's face or to assume the subordinate body language that stops the music.

Neuter your male dog before one year of age or as soon as both testicles drop. Overt dominance may not appear until he is two years old. Neutering reduces macho and roaming instincts. Be aware that testosterone levels take several months to decrease after neutering.

Spay your female. Breeding females can be instinctively more competitive around other females. A female in season should never be on the trail. She will create havoc, and her mating instincts will override her flawless obedience record of accomplishment for sure.

A leashed dog can be overly protective. Avoid stress by taking a detour around other hikers with dogs or stepping off the trail with your dog at a sit while the other hiker and dog walk by.

Do not panic at the hint of raised hackles and loud talk. Most of it is just posturing. If your dog is off-leash, keep walking away from the other dog while encouraging your dog to come in your most enthusiastic voice and with the promise of a biscuit. If

When unsure if other dogs are friendly, leash your dog and keep an upbeat, confident demeanor as you walk past.

she complies, reward her with a "good dog" and the promised biscuit for positive reinforcement.

Walking back toward the dogs, screaming and interfering before they resolve their conflict, can stoke the fires of a more serious brawl. If the squabble escalates into a dogfight, make sure you cover your arms and hands before trying to break it up. Pull the dogs by the tail, lift their hind legs off the ground, or throw water on them to distract them.

As a last resort, you may have to throw sand or dirt in the eyes of the one with the grip to pry her away. One hiker who uses a cane as a hiking stick reports breaking up a dogfight or two by slipping the crook of his cane under the dog collar or harness to drag the thug away.

Do not give treats to other hikers' dogs. Competition for food and protection of territory are the root of most dogfights.

LEAVE NO TRACE

As our exploding urban populations rush to retreat into the backcountry, our fragile and diminishing eco-systems are at greater risk of collapsing under the weight of our hiking boots. More people competing for the use of limited recreation areas leave dog owners vulnerable to criticism. So . . .

» Pack out everything you pack in.
» Do not leave dog scat on the trail. Bury it away from the trail and surface water. Or, better yet, carry plastic bags for removal.
» Hike only where dogs are permitted, and abide by the regulations posted.
» Stay on the trail and in designated campsites in heavily used or developed areas.
» Step lightly in more remote pristine areas.
» Do not let your dog chase wildlife.
» Do not let your dog charge other dogs or hikers, regardless of his harmless exuberance and friendly intentions. A leash is a great pacifier around people who may not be comfortable with dogs.
» Dogs can spook horses and pack stock, putting riders in a precarious situation. Step off the trail and wait with your dog at a sit position until the traffic has passed. Always leash your dog when passing other hikers, cyclists, horseback riders, or anyone with whom you are sharing the trail.

Use your *sit* and *stay* commands when horses pass by on the trail.

»   Don't let your dog bark at hikers, pack animals, wildlife, or the moon. It is intrusive to those who choose hiking as an escape to quiet and serenity.

»   Some hikers have strong opinions about why dogs should not be allowed in the backcountry. Let your dog be an ambassador by demonstrating his best backcountry behavior.

»   For more information visit LNT.org.

COMMUNICATING WITH YOUR DOG

Your dog's two ways of communicating with you are through body language and vocal sounds. Listen to what he is trying to tell you by paying attention to his changes in demeanor on the trail. He is giving you important information about how he feels physically and his concerns about what awaits around the bend.

Body Language

When everything is okay, your dog will have a light, relaxed sway and an energetic bounce in his step. Ears suddenly forward and tail up or raised hackles (hair standing up on the back of his neck or base of the tail) indicate tension and alertness triggered by a smell, sound, or sight.

Vocal Communication

If your dog appears uneasy, hyperactive, and alert and begins to bark, growl, or whine, she could be sensing a possible threat. The unusual smell, sound, or sight may not be noticed by you, but respect her concern.

Learn to read your dog's body language for changes from perky to fatigued.

Stop, listen, and look around. Pat your dog and speak to her reassuringly while keeping your wits about you. Make sure your dog is leashed, and proceed cautiously until you identify the source of her concern, which can be as simple as another hiker around the bend or the presence of a rodent in the bushes.

Be Sensitive

Tail down, a stiff gait, and a lethargic pace may indicate a tightening of your dog's back or hip muscles from straining or bruising of soft tissue. Examine him carefully, checking his pads and between the toes for cuts or foreign bodies that could be causing him discomfort or pain. If he appears okay, stop and rest and make sure he gets water. He may need a snack to boost his energy.

If your dog looks drained, demoralized, or sick; is injured; or you cannot explain his odd behavior, trust that something is wrong. Dogs in general have an almost misplaced desire to please, even when in pain. Be considerate of your best friend's needs and limitations. Do not push him and jeopardize his well-being to meet your expectations and goals. On the trail you are a team and your teammate depends on you. Alter the route, and when in doubt, cut the excursion short. In the unfortunate event that there is something serious going on with your dog, you may have to carry him out. You want to share safe, positive experiences that will nurture your enthusiasm for hiking.

Be realistic and sensitive to your dog's physical condition and morale, or you may be carrying him home.

On the other hand, fatigue at the end of the day is normal. A mellow dog after a solid day's work and play on the trail is a good thing. After a meal and a good night's rest, your dog should emerge refreshed in the morning. If he's dragging, take it easy by hiking a shorter distance to your next campsite or making extra rest stops on the way to the car if this is the end of the trip. (See Chapter Nine for suggested treatment of sore muscles.)

PREVENTIVE CARE

Let your dog's pace determine the pace of the hike. Keep her on-leash during the first thirty minutes of the hike. Off-leash fresh out of the starting gate, she may run around in a burst of energy and tucker herself out too soon because she has no way of knowing to pace herself.

Stop frequently for water breaks, and use the stops to examine your dog from head to tail. Remove the pack and check for chafing. Run your hands along her body, feeling for foxtails and burrs before they become a problem. Check her feet for worn pads and foreign bodies lodged between the toes.

WILDLIFE CONFLICTS

Most hikers with dogs come to the natural world "in peace" to retreat and absorb the beauty. Nevertheless, you are still an uninvited guest at best. Respect the animals whose home you are in, and trespass lightly.

Protecting Wildlife

Leashes are mandatory in many outdoor recreation areas primarily to protect the wildlife that lives, breeds, migrates, or nests there. Even in areas where your dog is allowed off-leash, do not let him chase wildlife or livestock for sport. It stresses and depletes the animal of survival energy and can cause a serious injury that leads to a cruel, agonizing death.

In the spring, nesting birds are very vulnerable to free-roaming dogs in meadows and low brush. Young deer can be separated from their mothers and fall prey to your dog's primal but inappropriate impulses.

Your companion is more likely to chase wildlife at the beginning of the hike, when he is fresh out of the starting gate. Keep him on-leash for about thirty minutes while he walks off some of his excess energy and gets used to his surroundings. If you have any doubts about your dog's behavior, keep him leashed.

Preventing Encounters

The potential for being injured or killed by a wild animal is extremely low when compared to many other natural hazards. Information and preparedness is the safest way for hikers with dogs to enjoy their time on the trail. Although there is no absolute rule to wild animal behavior, there is sufficient knowledge to trust some established guidelines.

When given the opportunity, most wild animals are more than happy to avoid humans; unfortunately, people often feed wild animals because they look cute and cuddly. Once a wild animal gets a taste of human food, it becomes habituated to that food and will not forget that humans are a source of food. Wild animals that have grown accustomed to human food and garbage can become brazen, posing a threat to human safety.

Bears and Bear Safety

Development encroaching on habitat and more hikers in remote wilderness areas have increased the bear's exposure to humans, their food, and their garbage. In bears, these bad human-engendered habits identify them as "problem" bears, which leads to their eventual and inevitable destruction. If you love wild animals, respect them, admire them from a safe distance, and do not feed them. A fed bear is a dead bear.

There is no scientific evidence that dogs are "bear bait." But a loose dog in bear country runs more of a chance of antagonizing a bear that is protecting her cubs. Even if your dog gets lucky and runs back to you unharmed, your problems are just beginning if the bear follows.

Bear Facts

» Bears can run, swim, and climb trees.
» Bears have good vision, excellent hearing, and a superior sense of smell.
» Bears are curious and attracted to food smells.
» Bears can be out at any time of day but are most active in the coolness of dawn and dusk and after dark.
» Bears and wild animals in general prefer anonymity. If they know you are out there, they will avoid your path.

It is a privilege to see a bear along the trail, but remain vigilant.

Stay on the trail, where there are fewer chances of surprising a bear snacking in a berry patch. Make your presence known with noise that is distinctly man-made, such as talking, singing, or humming a tune. The slight jingle of a metal ID tag against the metal rabies tag acts like a bell on your dog's collar or harness and can help notify bears of your presence. A small bell on the dog collar and one on your belt, walking stick, or boot lace is a stronger statement in grizzly country.

When it comes to odor, in bear country the motto is "less is safer." Pack all food items (human and dog) and any other odorous items in airtight resealable bags. Dispose of all items with food smells in airtight bags, in bear-proof storage containers. Clean your dishes and pet bowls. Some national forests and wilderness areas require that campers use plastic, portable, bear-resistant food canisters. These canisters (some collapsible) are available for sale or rent at sporting goods stores and some ranger stations.

If you see a bear in the distance, stop, stay calm, and don't run. Keep your dog close to your side on-leash. You should feel awe rather than panic. Walk a wide upwind detour so the animal can get your scent, and make loud banging or clanging noises as you leave the area. If the bear is at closer range, the same principles apply while you keep your eye on the bear and back down the trail slowly if the terrain doesn't allow you to negotiate a detour.

Avoid sudden movements that could spook or provoke the bear. Be cool and slow but deliberate as you make your retreat. To learn more about hiking in bear country, refer to *Backpacker* magazine's *Bear Country Behavior,* Bill Schneider (FalconGuides, 2012).

Mountain Lions

There are fewer mountain lions than bears, and the mountain lion population is concentrated in the western United States and Canada. As with bears, development and human intrusion are at the core of encounter problems.

>> Keep your dog on-leash on the trail.
>> Keep your dog in the tent at night.

- » Seeing doesn't mean attacking. If you come across a mountain lion, stay far enough away to give it the opportunity to avoid you.
- » Do not approach or provoke the lion.
- » Walk away slowly, and maintain eye contact. Running will stimulate the lion's predatory instinct to chase and hunt.
- » Make yourself big by putting your arms above your head and waving them. Raise your jacket or walking stick above your head to appear bigger. Do not bend down or make any motion that will make you look or sound like easy prey.
- » Shout and make noise.
- » If necessary, walking sticks can be weapons, as can rocks or anything you can get your hands on to fight back with.

Mountain Lion Facts

- » Mountain lions are elusive, and preying on humans is uncharacteristic.
- » Mountain lions are most active at dawn and dusk and usually hunt at night.
- » They are solitary and secretive and require a vegetated habitat for camouflage while they stalk prey.
- » Their meal of choice is big game (deer, bighorn sheep, and elk). In the absence of game, however, they can make a meal of domestic livestock or small mammals.
- » Mountain lions feed on what they kill. An unattended dog in camp is far more appetizing than his kibble.

For more information on hiking in mountain lion country, refer to *Mountain Lion Alert* by Steven Torres (FalconGuides, 1997).

Other Animals

Bobcats

Smaller than mountain lions, these wild cats are no threat to humans and would prefer climbing a tree over confronting your dog.

Wolves

Even if there were enough wolves that you might have the privilege of seeing one, the few that are left live and hunt in packs as their ancestors did, and they stay far away from humans. I have had the unexpected privilege of watching a pack of four wolves cross the trail just yards ahead of me while hiking in the Laurentides region of Québec at dawn. Stealthy, lithe, and almost ghostlike, they floated across the trail single file and oblivious to the two human observers.

Coyotes

In spite of their ability to survive persecution in healthier numbers than their wolf cousins, coyotes are rarely a threat to you on the trail. Nevertheless, letting your dog follow a coyote in the woods can end badly for the dog.

Skunks and Porcupines

Skunks and porcupines are primarily nocturnal and will fend off the curious with a spray or shot of barbed needles, respectively. A dog pierced by a mask of porcupine quills is a pitiful sight. Few dogs can withstand the pain of having barbed needles pulled out of their face by inexperienced, nervous hands without any anesthetic. Take your dog to a vet as quickly as possible.

Snakes

Most dogs have an instinctive aversion to lizards and snakes, and will jump away at the first sight, sound, or touch of a slither. Snakebites are usually the result of stepping on a snake unknowingly rather than conscious provocation. Most snakebites occur on the nose or front legs and can be lethal to a small or young dog. If taken to the vet quickly, larger adult dogs will survive the majority of bites. Ask your veterinarian if the recently developed rattlesnake vaccine would benefit your dog. Ask your vet or local dog club about snake avoidance classes in your area. (See Chapter Nine for treatment of venomous bites.)

Chapter Nine

Trail Nuisances, Emergencies, and First Aid

FOXTAILS

These arrow-like grasses are at their worst in late summer and early fall, when they are dry, sharp, and just waiting to burrow in some dog's fuzzy coat. The dry foxtail can be inhaled by a dog, lodge itself in the ear canal or between the toes, or camouflage itself in the dog's undercoat, puncturing the skin and causing infection. Foxtails have the potential to cause damage to vital organs.

Inspect your dog's ears and toes and run your hands through his coat, inspecting under the belly, legs, and tail. Brush out his coat after excursions where there were even hints of foxtails. Violent sneezing and snorting is an indication he may have inhaled a foxtail. Even if the sneezing or shaking decreases in intensity or frequency, the foxtail can still be tucked where it irritates only occasionally while it travels deeper, causing more serious damage. Take your dog to a vet as soon as possible. He may have to be anesthetized to remove the foxtail.

POISON IVY, OAK, AND SUMAC

Poison ivy and poison oak are three-leaved vine or bush plants ranging from green to red depending on the season. Poison sumac is a shrub or small tree (up to 30 feet tall) with seven to thirteen leaves on a branch. These plants can cause topical irritations on hairless areas of your dog's body. (You can apply cortisone cream to the affected area.) Find out if there is poison ivy (usually in the eastern states), poison oak (mainly in the western states), or poison sumac where you plan to hike, and make sure you wash your hands with soap after handling your dog. The resin can rub off your dog onto you, your sleeping bag, your car seat, and your furniture at home.

If you are very sensitive to these rashes, bathe your dog after the hike, and sponge your arms and legs with diluted chlorine bleach or Tecnu soap or anti-itch spray, an outdoor cleanser that removes plant oil from your skin. Tecnu soap also can be used on your laundry.

OTHER POISONOUS PLANTS

Unfortunately, your dog may be tempted to taste and chew hazardous plants. This includes plants found in your backyard, like rhubarb. In the wilderness there are similar dangers—plants such as rhododendrons and Japanese yew may cause considerable sickness and discomfort for your pet.

If you suspect poisoning, take note of what your dog ate and head back to the car. Once out of the woods, call your vet or an animal poison control center. (See Appendix B for phone numbers.)

FLEAS AND TICKS

Fleas are uncomfortable for your dog and carry tapeworm eggs, and ticks are one of nature's most painfully potent and tenacious creatures for their size. Some tick bites cause uncomfortable red, swollen irritation to the area of the skin where they attach and can make the area feel like it was pounded with a two-by-four. In some cases, tick bites can inflict temporary paralysis. Other types of ticks carry Rocky Mountain spotted fever and Lyme disease, the latter of which is reported to be the most common tick-carried disease in the United States.

Check yourself and your dog regularly to remove ticks before they bite.

Where Do Dogs Get Ticks?

Ticks thrive on wild hosts (deer are the most common) around lakes, streams, meadows, and some wooded areas. They cling to the unsuspecting hiker or dog. On dogs, they crawl out of the fur and attach to the skin around the neck, face, ears, stomach, or any soft, fleshy cavity. They attach to their hosts by sticking their mouthparts into the skin to feed on the host's blood and swell up until they dangle from the skin like an ornament.

Removing a Tick

1. Try not to break off any mouthparts (remaining parts can cause infections), and avoid getting tick fluids on you through crushing or puncturing the tick.

2. Pinch the tick at the base of the skin and twist as you pull it.

3. Grasp the tick as close to the skin as possible with blunt forceps, tweezers, or with your fingers in rubber gloves, tissue, or any barrier to shield your skin from possible tick fluids.

4. Remove the tick with a steady pull.

5. After removing the tick, disinfect the skin with alcohol and wash your hands with soap and water.

There is an abundance of chemical and natural flea and tick products on the market, including collars, dips, sprays, powders, pills, and oils. Some products have the advantage of being effective on both fleas and ticks, remain effective on wet dogs, and require an easy once-a-month topical application. Consult your veterinarian about a safe and appropriate product.

MOSQUITOES

Avon's Skin So Soft is a less-toxic and more pleasant-smelling—though not as effective—mosquito repellent than repellents containing DEET. Mix one cap of the oil with one pint of water in a spray bottle. Spray your dog and run your hands through her coat from head to toe and tail to cover her with a light film of the mixture. Be careful to avoid her eyes and nostrils, but do not miss the outer ear areas. Organic solutions containing eucalyptus can also be used as a mosquito repellent.

Besides being annoying, mosquitoes carry heartworm. Consult your veterinarian about preventive medication.

BEES, WASPS, HORNETS, AND YELLOW JACKETS

A leash is the best preventive measure to protect your dog from her own curiosity. Insect nests can be in trees or on the ground.

TRAIL EMERGENCIES AND TREATMENT

Planning, a commonsense approach, and a leash will help prevent most mishaps on the trail. Keep your dog on-leash when

>> hiking in territory known for its higher concentration of specific hazards (bears, mountain lions, snakes, skunks);

>> crossing fast-moving streams;

>> negotiating narrow mountainside trails;

>> hiking in wind and snow (dogs can become disoriented and lose their way).

If your dog gets into trouble, following are some basic first-aid treatments you can administer until you can get him to a vet.

Bleeding from Cuts or Wounds

1. Remove any obvious foreign object.

2. Rinse the area with warm water or 3 percent hydrogen peroxide.

3. Cover the wound with clean gauze or cloth and apply firm, direct pressure over the wound for about ten minutes to allow clotting to occur and bleeding to stop.

4. Place a nonstick pad or gauze over the wound, and bandage with gauze wraps (the stretchy, clingy type). For a paw wound, cover the bandaging with a bootie. (An old

Be ready for trail emergencies with a basic first-aid kit.

sock with duct tape on the bottom is a good bootie substitute. Use adhesive tape around the sock to prevent it from slipping off; be careful not to strangle circulation.)

Insect Bites

Bee stings and spider bites may cause itching, swelling, and hives. If the stinger is still present, scrape it off with your nail or tweezers at the base away from the point of entry. (Pressing the stinger or trying to pick it from the top can release more toxins.)

Apply a cold compress to the area, and spray it with a topical analgesic like Benadryl to relieve the itch and pain. As a precaution, carry an over-the-counter antihistamine (again, such as Benadryl) and ask your vet about the appropriate dosage before you leave, in case your dog has an extreme allergic reaction with excessive swelling.

Venomous Bites (Spiders, Snakes, and Scorpions)

Dogs often startle venomous critters when they dig under rocks or fallen logs. If your dog is bitten by a spider, snake, or scorpion,

» Keep your dog calm (activity stimulates the absorption of venom).
» Rinse the area with water, and transport your dog to the nearest vet.

Skunked

When your dog gets skunked, a potent, smelly cloud of spray burns his eyes and makes his mouth foam. The smell can make you gag, and contact with the spray on your dog's coat can give your skin a tingling, burning sensation. Apply de-skunking shampoo as soon as possible.

It's a good idea to carry lemon juice concentrate and a pair of disposable latex gloves (available in hardware store paint departments) in your pack. A lemon juice rub and stream water rinse will tone down some of the fumes until you can give your pooch a full spa treatment—with a de-skunking shampoo mix—at a pet wash location, groomer, veterinarian, or in your own backyard.

Always carry a couple of dog towels or old sheets in your car to wrap your dog and protect your upholstery. In a pinch, large plastic trash bags and duct tape come in handy to create a barrier between the seats and a damp, stinky dog.

De-skunking Shampoo Mix

» 1 quart 3% hydrogen peroxide
» 1/4 cup baking soda
» 1 tablespoon dish soap
» Put on rubber gloves and thoroughly wet your dog, apply mixture, and let stand for fifteen minutes. Rinse and repeat as needed. It will help, but only time, air, and repeated bathing will put distance between you and the stench.

Heatstroke

Heatstroke occurs when a dog's body temperature rises rapidly above 104ºF and panting is ineffective to regulate temperature.

1. Get your dog out of the sun and begin reducing body temperature (no lower than 103ºF) by applying water-soaked towels on her head (to cool the brain), chest, abdomen, and feet.

2. Let your dog stand in a pond, lake, or stream while you gently pour water on her. Avoid icy

Standing in a stream cools an overheated dog.

water—it can chill her. Swabbing the foot-pads with alcohol will help.

Frostbite

Frostbite is the freezing of a body part exposed to extreme cold. Tips of ears and pads are the most vulnerable.

1. Remove your dog from the cold.
2. Apply a warm compress to the affected area without friction or pressure.

Hypothermia

Hypothermia occurs when a dog's body temperature drops below 95°F because of overexposure to cold weather, which can happen in dry, wet, or snowy conditions.

1. Take the dog indoors or into a sheltered area where you can make a fire.

2. Wrap him in a blanket, towel, sleeping bag, your clothing, or whatever you have available. If available, wrap him in warm towels or place warm water bottles in a towel next to him.

3. Hold him close to you for body heat.

Sore Muscles

1. Rest your dog.

2. Apply cold-water compresses to tight muscle areas to reduce inflammation.

3. Administer Ascriptin, a buffered aspirin (check with your vet on dosage for your dog's breed and weight).

Cardiopulmonary Resuscitation

Check with your veterinarian or local humane society for pet CPR classes.

Chapter Ten
Public Lands and Dogs

National forests offer scenery as stunning as national parks, and dogs are welcome on backcountry trails.

Hike on BLM lands if you want off-leash solitude.

Stop by the visitor center for current information about dog-friendly trails on the lands you plan to hike.

ADA

The United States and Canada have an increasing number of ADA-accessible trails so disabled hikers can enjoy getting off the beaten track and connecting to nature with their companion dog. Companion dogs have the advantage of being allowed on national park trails as well as all public places and public transportation worldwide.

ADA-accessible trails allow the disabled and their companion dogs to enjoy nature up close.

Epilogue
See You on the Trail

There is no better playground than the great outdoors, and no better playmate than your dog. Plan, prepare, and safely share your best moments on the trail with your dog. Remember to pack the snacks, water, leash, good sense, and trail manners. Take good care of your hiking companion, and he or she will take care of you.

Revel in watching your dog's spirit soar on the trail.

APPENDIX A

CHECKLISTS (Hiking, Backpacking)

DAY HIKE

- ❏ Flea and tick treatment application prior to hike
- ❏ Bug repellent in sealed plastic bag
- ❏ Health and vaccination certificate
- ❏ Collar and bandanna or colorful harness with permanent and temporary ID tags and rabies tag
- ❏ Leash
- ❏ Plastic water containers full of water: 32-ounce bottle for half-day hike (under four hours) and 2-quart bottle for longer hikes
- ❏ Eight ounces of water per dog per hour or 3 miles of hiking
- ❏ Water purifier for full-day hike
- ❏ Snacks for you and your pet
- ❏ Collapsible dish or resealable bag
- ❏ Plastic bags for cleaning up after your dog
- ❏ Sunscreen for tips of ears and nose
- ❏ Booties for pooch and comfortable, sturdy, waterproof boots for you
- ❏ Wire grooming brush to help remove stickers and foxtails from your pet's coat
- ❏ Extra clothing: sweater or coat for a thin-coated dog
- ❏ Whistle

- ❏ Extra-large, heavy-duty plastic garbage bags (good to sit on and make a handy poncho in the rain)
- ❏ Flyers for a lost dog
- ❏ Pocketknife (Swiss Army–type knife that includes additional tools)
- ❏ Flashlight and extra batteries
- ❏ Matches or cigarette lighter and emergency fire starter
- ❏ First-aid kit
- ❏ Contact for closest veterinarian

BACKPACKING

All items on day hike checklist, plus the following:

- ❏ Extra leash or rope
- ❏ Dog pack
- ❏ Doggie bedroll (foam sleeping pad)
- ❏ Dog's favorite chew toy
- ❏ Dog food (number of days on the trail times three meals a day)
- ❏ Additional water in a 2-quart bottle
- ❏ Water purifier
- ❏ Dog snacks (enough for six rest stops per hiking day)
- ❏ Collapsible food and water dish (resealable bags)
- ❏ Nylon tie-out line in camp (expandable leash can be extra leash and tie-out rope)

APPENDIX B

FIRST-AID KIT

A basic first-aid kit will contain a first-aid book and items useful to you and your dog, with a few dog essentials.

- » Muzzle—the most loving dogs can snap and bite when in pain. Muzzles come in different styles and sizes to fit all dog nose shapes.
- » Ascriptin (buffered aspirin)—older dogs in particular may be stiff and sore at the end of a hike or a backpacking excursion. Consult your vet on the appropriate dosage.
- » Antidiarrheal agents and GI protectants: Pepto-Bismol 1–3ml/kg/day; Kaopectate 1–2 ml/kg every 2–6 hours
- » Indigestion and stomach upset: Pepcid (famotidine) decreases gastric acid secretions, 0.1–2 mg/kg every 12–24 hours
- » Scissors (rounded tips) to trim hair around a wound
- » Hydrogen peroxide (3%) to disinfect surface abrasions and wounds
- » Antiseptic ointment
- » Gauze pads and gauze
- » Clingy and elastic bandages
- » Sock or bootie to protect a wounded foot

» Duct tape to wrap around the sole of sock used as a bootie
» Tweezers to remove ticks, needles, or foreign objects in a wound
» Styptic powder for bleeding
» Rectal thermometer
» Hydrocortisone spray to relieve plant rashes and stings
» One application of de-skunking shampoo mix (See Chapter Nine.)
» Phone numbers: your veterinarian's telephone number and number of the veterinary clinic closest to the trailhead; ASPCA National Animal Poison Control Center, (888) 426-4435 (tape the number inside your first-aid kit); American Veterinary Association, (800) 248-2862 (www.AVMA.org)

RESOURCES FOR POOCH GEAR AND TRAIL ACCESSORIES

- » Rei.com, outdoor gear cooperative
- » Petco.com, pet supply store
- » Petsmart.com, pet supply store
- » Petfoodexpress.com, pet supply store
- » wolfpacks.com, specializes in custom dog packs
- » ruffwear.com, manufacturer of dog gear and accessories
- » Topographic maps: www.natgeomaps.com/outdoormaps.html; store.usgs.gov

A dog at your side will enrich the endless adventures on the trails ahead.

WEBSITES FOR RESOURCES

» *AAA PetBook,* aaa.com/petbook. Membership in the American Automobile Association (AAA) gives you access to tour books and campground maps (free of charge) for every US state and Canadian province. Each tour book includes a list and map of national, state, and other recreational areas, including a chart indicating which have hiking trails that allow pets on-leash; (800) JOIN-AAA.

» workingdogs.com (articles and studies)

» baywoof.com (articles)

» bringfido.com (pet-friendly travel advice)

» nacsw.net (National Association of Canine Scent Work)

» Google "hiking club dogs" with name of the city, county, or state.

» Google "dog friendly hiking trails" or "ADA accessible hiking trails" by county or state.

» usgs.gov

» projectcoyote.org

INDEX

ABOUT THE AUTHOR

Linda Mullally is a freelance writer and the author of three hiking guides, including *Best Hikes with Dogs: Central California,* 2008. She is also a travel columnist for the *Monterey Herald* and a "doggie nanny." She was the first travel columnist for *Dog Fancy* magazine, sharing information about dog-friendly getaways while promoting responsible dog ownership. When Linda and her attorney/photographer husband are not trekking in mountain kingdoms, they divide their time between Carmel, California, and the Eastern Sierra with Gypsy, a ten-year-old Australian Cattle Dog/Chihuahua mix they recently welcomed into their hearts and home. Linda also escorts groups on cruise ships with David, providing her with an opportunity to write about outdoor adventure possibilities in ports of call.